Monday Moments®

Footprints of Faith, Hope, and Love

Monday Moments®

Footprints of Faith, Hope, and Love

A curated collection of entries from the
popular *Monday Moments* Blog

ANN HALES

TOP READS PUBLISHING, INC

VISTA, CALIFORNIA

First Edition

ISBN: 978-0-9986838-4-3 (hardcover)

Library of Congress Control Number: 2017963991

Monday Moments is published by: Top Reads Publishing, Inc., 1035 E. Vista Way, Suite 205, Vista, CA, 92084-4213 USA

For information please direct emails to:
topreadspublishing@gmail.com or visit the website:
www.TopReadsPublishing.com

Cover design, book layout and typography: Teri Rider & Associates
Interior Photos: Ann Hales
Cover, author photos, and photos on pages 73, 102: Rachel Leigh

Printed in Canada

25 24 23 22 21 20 19 18   1 2 3 4 5 6 7 8 9

DEDICATION

In loving memory of my beautiful mother, Fern Heaton Lawhead, I dedicate this book. Her rich legacy of grace, love, courage, kindness and dignity lives on for my brother and me, and her precious grandchildren and great grandchildren. I have felt her comforting encouragement every day since we said goodbye, whether I have been taking care of my family, mastering the art of making her famous lemon meringue pie (my dad's favorite), or writing this book. She was a sterling influence in my life and many of her fine examples are woven throughout the pages of this book.

The Beginning

Hello! I warmly welcome you to *Monday Moments*. It has been written just for you.

We will slowly wander through the pages together, holding close those thoughts that speak to us. I have come to know and to appreciate over the years that trials are the metal that build our character, if we let them. None of us are immune to difficult times, some more life changing and challenging than others. Many years ago, I learned important advice on surviving such times from a dear and wise friend. He told me I had a choice. I could dissolve into the ashes of despair and unfairness or rise up and go forward, with everything in me to do the best I could. Thankfully, I chose the latter. I also came to know that prayer is the stepping stone to God's guiding light as we are making our way through. Patience, comfort, peace, courage and eventual answers will be illuminated during such times. When we come out the other side of our tribulations we are better for them, and we will have grown in ways we never thought possible.

At the true core of every story whether fiction or nonfiction lies its purpose for being told. It is a time when the reader finds a connection with the author on some common level. The book I have written is full of optimism and promise, hope, faith and a disposition of never giving up. Each chapter is based on what I have lived and have found to be true and guiding in my life. I am hopeful that we will meet somewhere within the pages of this book, like good friends. As many of us have, I grew up believing in happily-ever-afters. Over the years, I have come to realize that it is what each one of us creates that is not only our own happy ending, but all that happens in-between.

It was my dream to have a forever marriage and eventually be embracing my children's spouses and grandchildren through our welcoming front door, and into our home and into our hearts. It was the end of summer 1992, and this is where my story begins. The moving van had come and gone. I was left alone in my dream home with my thoughts, my memories and, my tears. On that warm summer night I walked from room to room, pausing in each to seal in my heart every remembrance, tender and happy. As I did so, I closed my eyes and shut the door of each of my five children's bedrooms as if somehow, magically, it would all be okay. But, as I was to find out, it was not meant to be. Sometimes, when there is a storm brewing, it starts slowly. Perhaps I was just too numb to see that the wind had begun rustling in the trees and the storm was on its way. As I shut our front door for the final time, I knew I would never again hear the familiar sounds of our family there. A new and uncertain chapter was unfolding. Our little cottage was ready and waiting for our family, even our two collies were settled there. The only person that wasn't alright was me, even though it looked that way on the outside.

The drive from La Canada, California to Balboa Island that August night seemed like an eternity, even though it was just a little over an hour away. I could not wait to see my children asleep in their beds in the cozy cottage that we would now call home. My head was spinning with so much emotion, and too many questions without answers. I knew it was going to be up to me to keep everyone alright in our new city and school beginning for the year, just around the corner. That was my calling. I was their mom. I was soon to find out there are many ways to make a home as we settled into our tiny place on the Island. I remember those first few weeks as vividly as if it was yesterday. The smell of salt air so thick and pungent I could taste it. The sounds of boats pitching and creaking in the bay and barking seals greeting me on my early morning walks around this precious island. The fragrance in the air that announced a storm was about to blow in, was yet another sign to me that I was getting in touch with a fuller meaning of life. I was reaching out and embracing the intangible... sights, smells and sounds that I would grow to love as my security, over the next six years. My personal journey was only just beginning on this beloved island we now called home.

In what seems like a lifetime ago, I wonder at times, actually many times, how we all got through those years. Divorce is not easy on a family, it is actually devastating. And yet, I do know how we made it through. It was God's outstretched hand, His grace shining on me and my family, having faith in each new day with the circumstances that would confront us, and never ending prayers. Sometimes, when it seems you can't take another step or another breath, God is getting ready to give you strength and growth in yet another area of your life. This was to be His plan for me. After I became the sole parent and support of my five children it seemed as if it was one mountain to climb after another. Often the valleys were full of the hardest challenges and lessons. At the end of most adversity, when you allow it, a shining character usually emerges due to the humility you have learned coming through it. That became my mantra as I prayed that perhaps one day all that I had learned, might be written in a book to help others. That day has sweetly come.

This is a true story, one that will be laced with inspiration and warmth in each chapter, representing what I have learned, lived and loved along the way. You may experience some tears and smiles as you relate things I have written but most of all, I pray my story will fill you with hope. As life presents us with many different circumstances, it is hope that will fill our lamps with light to shine on our paths and see us through. At the time my "journey" began I never dreamed I would write a book! It was all I could do to manage each day, the family I was raising, and my own jobs to support us. When I looked at the big mountain in front of me, it seemed unimaginable that I would ever climb to the top. But what I was to learn, was that there were many twists and turns to get there. It was a good thing I did not know all that was to lie ahead of me in the valleys with five children to love, feed, clothe, comfort and educate. I vividly remember in those quiet moments late at night, my prayers, many times pleading to God. These prayers gave me hope and strengthened my faith as I awoke each morning, and was given yet another helping of courage to do it all over again. Taking one day at a time, turned into months and into years and eventually comprised five high school graduations, five college graduations, three weddings, and finally turned me into "Mimi" (grandmother to five beautiful grandchildren). There is a great and sterling truth in "one day at a time." When we worry too much about more than the day we are in, we rob that day of its energy and joy. Whether the next day is full of sweet surprises or full of sadness or tragedy, is unforeseen. I learned to cherish the moments in each day and the lessons I learned, as no two days are ever the same. I also learned that no matter what comes our way each day, there is a hidden gift, one we can look at or unwrap, and use it for our good. In those more difficult years as well as today, almost always, those gifts are my family and my friends who always bring me joy, support and love.

You might be asking yourself where all of this inspiration came from! Simply put, from years of writing to family and friends from my heart, whether it was celebrating a special day through my heartfelt words, a note of encouragement in a lunch sack to one of my children during elementary school years, a sympathy card, journaling, letters of comfort and inspiration to my college-age children or, just because. Little did I know that years of those "writings" would develop into something greater. In the summer of 2009, *Monday Moments* was born on a sandy beach on Balboa Island, California. On that sunny summer day I happened to be there comfortably reading a book, when my youngest son rode his bike over to visit me. During our conversation, his encouragement and enthusiasm for me to continue writing and inspire others sparked a real sincere interest in me. I always felt the experiences in my life thus far had not been by chance. The insight I had gained was a gift and the opportunity to write and share with others, a great blessing. My thoughts turned to writing a weekly inspirational thought, and quickly its name became very clear to me. From my beach chair that very day, and with notebook and pen in hand, my heart and mind became one and took flight on an inspirational journey. Along with this was uncompromising love, enthusiasm and encouragement from my family, friends and soon my *Monday Moments* audience, for whom I will be forever grateful.

At first, I began with more simple thoughts sent out by email every Monday morning, true to the values and the simplicity of life I believe in. I have always seen the glass as half full and most of my writings have this inflection. When often times the negatives in the world seem to surround us, I strive to give my reading audience something more tangible to believe in and hope for. The many thoughts I have written and will continue to write and share, are written with much love, understanding, compassion, humor, tenderness and devotion. I believe these thoughts run as a common thread through all of us. It is my hope that in the following chapters the spirit of love, hope, and faith will embrace you and bring you home again.

So, where do we begin as we take this inspirational voyage together? Whether you are in a season of prosperity and joy or down in the deepest valley, my prayer is that you will find peace, inspiration, and hope. A dear friend and author, Annie Quinn, gave me sage advice when she told me to write from my heart. And so, come with me as I have done just that. I am grateful that my personal journey wasn't all for naught. It is very clear to me that I experienced all I did in those years, to be able to give back throughout the pages in this book I have written for you. Throughout the chapters I have penned, you will find experiences, emotions, values, memories, stories, and many doses of hope and faith... all of which I have lived.

CHAPTER ONE ♡ *Fine Things*

On September 15, 2014, I took a road trip through Central California. Through the winding cliffs of Big Sur and into Carmel, I was prepared to write the last page of my first book, intended solely for my family. This would be my Christmas gift to each one of my five children. It was to be a surprise and my legacy to each of them. As I look back on that final night in Carmel, it was magical and a dream come true. There, I wrote next to a crackling fire in the fireplace in a charming room I had rented, and snuggled next to me, my precious four-legged furry companion, Bailey.

I knew this was perhaps the most important page of all. It spoke from the depths of my heart of my deep abiding love for my beautiful children, my precious grandchildren, my loving parents, my amazing and caring brother, my cherished friends, and my deep faith in God, and His unwavering love for us as a family. The many celebrations, memories and treasures, largely of the heart, shine ever so brightly in my mind. Over the years, you too, will know what the truly choice things are in your own lives and how family, friends, and memories will leave sterling imprints on your heart, as they have on my own. There is an essential element of peace, contentment and happiness knowing these fine things in our lives are genuine and exceptional, and are the most important ones after all.

CHAPTER TWO ♥ *The Simplicity Of The Sea*

When summertime arrives each year, I find myself reaching again for one of my favorite books, *Gifts from the Sea*. Its inspirational author and devoted mother, Anne Morrow Lindbergh, found her greatest writing while alone, in a little cottage on the beach. Once there, her soul soared with the ocean and what it had to teach her... patience and the importance of living in grace. I too, am drawn to the beach and to the ever rolling waves, where over the years I have found my greatest peace, and the simplicity in the answers, to the questions of my heart. Yes, the sea is always giving to us and when we seek her out, and have patience, she will deliver the gifts we need most.

CHAPTER THREE ♥ *A Simple Voyage*

One does not have to travel very far to find the cream of the voyage. It may just be the pure enjoyment of the adventure in leaving certain things behind and moving forward into new chapters in one's life. This alone can hold inspiring significance. Welcoming each new day, our footprints continue to etch more of our earthly journey. When we wonder when we'll "arrive" it is wise and comforting to remember that life is not only about the destination, but all the roads of memory in between. The lessons we learn along the way prepare us to be stronger, more compassionate, loving, and forgiving travelers. Often, the greatest pearl found is looking inward and finding pure contentment in where we are, and who we have become.

CHAPTER FOUR ♥ *A Welcoming Beacon*

Over a year ago, God's grace through a dear friend brought me back to Balboa Island. I am so grateful to live on this enchanted isle in a charming cottage, and drink in her restorative gifts every day. Most Saturday mornings you will find me strolling there. I always enjoy the delicious aroma in the chilly winter air of cinnamon rolls baking, the familiar smell of fireplaces burning from cozy nearby cottages, the friendly faces I greet on my walk, paddle boarding on the bay, and the high pitched "hello" from seagulls flying overhead. These simple gifts help inspire and invigorate me for all I am thinking about, while I wait on matters of my heart to reveal themselves. This sweet island is a welcoming beacon to me and my family, and where life happened to bring us. We never know what circumstances in our lives will change our surroundings and help us to bloom in places we may have never dreamed. Wherever your special place may be, it will call out to you. And, it will be a respite for you to ponder your thoughts and matters of your own heart. None of us know what lies ahead, but what I have experienced is that the comfort of familiarity brings peace to the soul, whether you are healing or just needing your memorable place.

CHAPTER FIVE ♥ *Faith*

Thus far on my life's journey, with the experiences and trials I have met along the way, I know the following to be true. Faith is looking at the bend in the road seeing no further, but believing there is more road ahead that will get us to our destination. To believe and to have faith in what lies ahead is woven in God's ultimate plan for all of us, as we face the challenges and new opportunities in life. There is great comfort in exercising this faith, for it is then God is taking us by the hand, and revealing there is truly more road ahead.

CHAPTER SIX ♡ *Living Thankfully*

When your arms are open in gratitude and your heart is full of hope, the abundance that will come is a gift and a blessing, and even a miracle, that will leave an imprint on your soul forever. It is the golden thread that ties our hearts together. As we live thankfully, our Heavenly Father will pour out even more blessings upon us. Many years ago my oldest son Brett, then a senior in high school, suffered a traumatic basketball injury to one of his legs. It happened to be during the years when we did not have health insurance, and I knew we were living on borrowed time before we would drastically need it. That day had come. Soon after x-rays were taken, three orthopedic surgeons walked into the examination room where we were waiting. Solemnly they delivered the diagnosis of Compartment Syndrome. One of the surgeons continued that unless my son went into surgery within a couple of hours, he would lose his leg. I still remember how I felt that day as his mother, especially knowing we were in the financial position we were. All humility left me as I picked up the phone and called the doctor I was working for at the time. I asked him if he could loan me the money I needed to get my son into the hospital. And, he did and he never asked for repayment. I promised I would pay the surgeon in two days, and at that moment, I had no idea how or where the money would come from. I only knew my word was good. The gifted surgeons saved my son's leg and tears of gratitude rushed down my face in the waiting room as they told me. I prayed to God so reverently and thanked Him for His tender mercy and for all the angels that stepped in to help us at that time. I knew somehow I would be able to pay the surgeon, and it came in the form of my tax return on the day I told him I would deliver a check to him. I was only short one hundred dollars! Yes, I know the power of prayer and the miracles that come into our lives when we need them most. Some experiences never leave us and that is dearly one of mine. Being thankful reminds us to live thankfully, and brings forth a harvest of emotions to our hearts and souls.

CHAPTER SEVEN ♡ *Live Your Life Now*

Over the past several years, I have been an active participant in the AVON Breast Cancer Walks to help end this disease. I lost my beautiful mother to breast cancer many years ago and it has become my crusade to help in any way I can. As I am writing this book I have just finished my fifth walk of 39 miles over two days. The walks are held in different major cities across the United States. It is an honor and a privilege to be a participant. I am grateful to the many wonderful supporters of this cause who have given generous donations so that I may walk. Each participant must raise eighteen hundred dollars. My goal is to complete three more walks over the next three years. It is typical for at least twenty-five hundred men and women to participate where a journey of hope, love and new friendships are made with the common bond to see an end to breast cancer. Opening and closing ceremonies always put a PINK ribbon around the weekend for me! The tenderness and reality of the personal stories shared always touch me deeply and make me wrap my arms around each day more firmly. One of the speakers, a survivor herself, shared this precious advice. She said, "So much in life is about waiting, whether it is waiting for answers to come in personal areas of our lives, dreams fulfilled, or possibly, waiting for a diagnosis." She continued, "Don't live your life waiting, live it fully now." I could not agree with her more, as I have seen how very fragile life can be. May God bless you and keep you well and happy, and may your days be full of the joy of *living life now.*

CHAPTER EIGHT ♡ *Birthdays*

The more years I celebrate, I have come to appreciate that our birthdays are Heaven's gifts! When we left our Heavenly home, we came here to experience all that would encompass our own unique lives. And, on that special day that is ours alone, we can enjoy being celebrated! Amidst the love, fun, and excitement, when we can stop and reflect and count our blessings, it makes that birthday even sweeter and the memories everlasting. A birthday I will remember into eternity was sadly, my mother's last one. She was in the final stages of pancreatic and stomach cancer. Nevertheless, she still wanted to celebrate by going out to lunch with me and to a movie she was looking forward to seeing. Even though my mom could not keep food down, by the grace of God's tender mercy, she was able to eat that day… and even a little popcorn afterwards at the movie. That was the last meal she ate until she passed away. I know God gave her that special day to be celebrated, and that is how I choose to remember my mom… full of grace and wanting one more lunch and movie with me. Thank you, Mom, for showing me courage and teaching me grace. I miss you.

CHAPTER NINE ♡ *Just Believe*

This magical time of the year is a season we all adore. Children, their wide eyes sparkling in sweet anticipation and excitement of what Santa Claus will bring is their purest way to believe. And for many, all over the world, to believe is a form of hope. Something so inspiring, warm, and beautiful is truly a gift from God to each one of us. I feel we are given this gift of hope in the month of December so that we will never stop believing. As we celebrate the birth of our Savior on Christmas Day, may we hold dearly His great love for each one of us, not only on this very special day, but throughout the year. His daily gifts of hope, love, and faith are wrapped in a multitude of magnificent ribbons so that we will always remember.

CHAPTER TEN *Make It Extraordinary*

We should all be grateful for those moments that keep us stepping higher and reaching for the best within ourselves. Our lives are full of hope, dreams, goals and some pretty fun adventures along the way! The human spirit teaches us to keep climbing, keep hoping, keep believing and loving, and never forget why we are here on this earth. Three years ago I was in the finishing stages of a book for my children, and it would become their legacy from me. I drove all the way to Big Sur, California to take a picture of its beautiful, rugged coastline, as I believe it is indeed extraordinary. I wanted them to remember that what we set our hearts and minds to achieve is possible.

If I was to give you one piece of advice as you make plans for your life, it would be, make it extraordinary. Have dreams, make plans, and follow them. Drink in everyday moments with lenses of gratitude, as often they will lead you to answers, miracles, and blessings just waiting to be discovered. And when you find them, cherish them. I have found throughout my life that when I begin my day with the intention of finding exceptional memorable moments, I usually do. It is then the inspiration comes and guides me to what is next, or finding peace and contentment just where I am. Remember, often it is not finding new places or things, it is finding "new eyes" that see things differently, defining you for being the best you can be. That, in itself, is living an extraordinary life.

CHAPTER ELEVEN ♡ *Trials*

A natural part of our existence is to encounter times of difficulty while we are here on this earth. The trials we face will be different for each one of us. If we let them, they can refine and strengthen our character in ways we would never have imagined. As I look back on many years ago and the worry of raising my family alone, I know I could have become bitter. Still, I did not want to be remembered that way in the eyes of my children or my friends. Trials too, can help enrich our faith for good things hoped for and not seen as quickly as we would like. From personal experience, my greatest comfort during such times is to stay close to God, trust in Him remaining full of faith, and taking one step and one day at a time. During the writing of this book my oldest daughter, Holly, was diagnosed with an inoperable brain aneurysm. When the news came it was deafening and numbing for weeks and weeks. The diagnosis of "inoperable" was not a word I could say or wrap my heart or head around, because it was happening to one of my children. As we prayed as a family and a family of friends, I was to more clearly understand that I had written about trials, but not one like this. God has a beautiful way of softening the most frightening diagnosis by giving us the gift of time to understand what is happening. Through the months, this beautiful daughter, wife and mother of four darling children, continues to walk through each day with faith and grace that there will be answers for her, and that our loving God will continue to hover ever near each and every day, bringing her tender mercies.

For each of you, I pray that your trials will be few. However, I know from my own experiences that our personal growth and character will be forever changed for good if the path we choose is to have faith, and climb the mountain before us with grace.

CHAPTER TWELVE ♡ *You Are Enough*

Not only are you enough, but you are more than enough! God has given each one of us our own unique gifts, talents, passions, challenges, strengths, perseverance, some weaknesses (enough to help us grow), and a generous helping of personality. In a world where there is so much competition, our humanness can often make us feel we may not measure up. Quite the contrary. When we find our passion and follow where it leads us, there will be our joy. With that joy will be the true knowledge that we are enough, and we are doing exactly what we are meant to do at this time in our lives.

CHAPTER THIRTEEN ♥ *The Red Sweatshirt*

Many years ago, on a cold and crisp December day, I had just finished buying Christmas greens at a local nursery. As I approached my car, I noticed her coming down the street. She was without a home, not much clothing and she was cold. Right away I glanced into my car, and my eyes fixed on a new red sweatshirt my children had just given me as an early Christmas present. It took me no more than a minute to know what I wanted to do. I reached for that priceless gift and with a kiss on its soft fabric, I walked towards my new friend. I said "Hello," wished her a Merry Christmas and told her I wanted her to be warm, and I gave her my sweatshirt. She gratefully accepted and held it close to her and said "thank you." It was a thank you born of much humility. I stood and watched her walk away until she was no longer in view. I prayed for her safety and that she would find warm shelter and a better life. That Christmas, around our little tree, I shared this story with my children. They were so happy their gift to me was able to help someone else. I thought of my new friend often throughout the coming year, until one day, my oldest daughter shared her beautiful story with me. She also lived in Newport Beach at that time, and had stopped at a nearby Starbuck's to buy some coffee before going to work. As she left with her coffee, she noticed a woman sitting outside wearing the same red sweatshirt my family had given to me… it was our Christmas friend. My daughter quickly turned around and went back into Starbuck's and bought her a large cup of hot coffee and presented it to her with love and a smile. Not many words were exchanged, just eyes that met, full of love and the warm sparkle of compassion. Our story had a special ending as it had come full circle. There is no particular season for giving. It can be any day, at any time, when the heart and an opportunity find each other.

A wish is a smile on

your heart

CHAPTER FOURTEEN ♡ *The Five Dollar Tree*

Many years ago my children and I moved into a home that needed a lot of love! After the interior was scrubbed, painted and shiny, it was time to pay attention to the front yard. I put a plan in place and visited a local nursery. After looking around at many different plants and trees, my eyes were drawn to a small tree that was about to be thrown away. It was then I heard a gruff voice say rather loudly, "Lady, if you want it, the tree is five dollars." I gently picked up the little tree, paid the cashier and drove home with a big smile on my face. In my heart I knew that little tree would grow to be the prettiest tree in our neighborhood! And, as the years passed by it was, and had grown to be the tallest Liquid Amber tree I had ever seen. In life we can never judge the small things. Within them there is a wonderful lesson to learn. Now, over twenty years later I often drive down that quaint little street and glance at that healthy, beautiful tree and I am reminded of the lesson it taught me. Sometimes the smallest things in life can make the biggest impact.

CHAPTER FIFTEEN ♡ *A Journey Through Healing*

For anyone that has ever suffered from an illness, an accident, loss of a loved one, or perhaps extreme sadness from a broken heart, some kind of healing will always take place at one time or another. Having experienced many of these myself and with my loved ones, I know this to be true. Each one of us will find our own unique path to follow as we heal. When we are patient and have faith, and when we connect our mind, body and soul and let them flow in unison together, our healing is well on its way. Every journey is a personal one and when we have come through it, we will emerge stronger than we ever believed possible, and we will personally know how to help someone else during their time of need.

CHAPTER SIXTEEN ♥ *Miracles*

Every day we hear of a miracle in some form, and perhaps we have been blessed enough to witness some of our own. Due to unforeseen circumstances, miracles may not always appear as soon as we would like them. We may also hear of wonders that seem to proceed a miracle. My personal favorites are rainbows and butterflies. And such it is with other wonders that appear before us, bringing us a feeling of awe and amazement. As we embrace patience, faith, and prayer while waiting, it can be the little moments that shine the brightest. It is my wish that you will have many little moments that will bring you hope while you wait.

CHAPTER SEVENTEEN ♡
Love Waiting On My Front Porch

It had been a long day at the office, and I was struggling with a nasty cold. Driving home, all I could envision was my pajamas and my warm, cozy bed! But, upon arriving home, as I walked closer to my welcoming front door, I saw LOVE wrapped in a brown paper bag on my front porch. Inside, was a freshly baked loaf of bread and a container of delicious chili. The angel that made me smile is a dear friend of mine, and she had known earlier in the day I was not feeling well. Her act of kindness brought home to me that when we receive gifts of the heart, it makes us continue to believe in moments like this… that love can be found everywhere, from the caring souls of others.

CHAPTER EIGHTEEN ♥ *Home*

The dictionary defines *home* as a place where a person lives. That is true for a basic definition, but a home is much, much more. Personally, over the course of my lifetime thus far, many places have been home to me, beginning with my childhood. Over time, my roots during those early years set the tone for the rest of my life and how I would celebrate traditions, friends and most of all, my family. I have had many opportunities to do just that, and I am grateful for the memories left in each one. I know this for sure, it is not the size of the home or its location, but the warmth and love that welcomes those I cherish through the door.

One of the many homes we have made, was the little cottage at 306 Ruby, Balboa Island. This is where we would call home for six years after moving from La Canada, as I mentioned earlier in my story. It was charming, sweet and inviting to all who walked through the door, and to us as a family who lived within its tiny walls. Bedtime was as simple as, "Good Night... I love you!" and everyone heard, as we were all so close together, but those were my memories. I loved those years.

During the first two years of living on the island, I had to rely heavily on my daughter Heather, who was then a junior at Corona del Mar High School. It was a lot to ask of her when she was trying to make new friends after just moving to this new school. Sometimes we don't have a choice, and have to call upon our children for their help. After her school day was over, she became mini Mom to her younger siblings until I got home from work. This involved homework, driving to dental and doctor's appointments, starting dinner and whatever else would come up during those hours I could not be at home. I will forever be grateful for her help during those years to anchor our home and family. Today, she is a wonderful wife and mother and has a beautiful little girl of her own. She got her experience early and it shows! Thank you Heather, with all of my heart, for being there when I could not. I love you.

CHAPTER NINETEEN ♥ *Two Hands*

In 2008, at my son's college graduation from Duke University, among the many talks given that ceremonious weekend, one stands out the strongest for me. It was delivered by Reverend Sam Wells. He relayed to the students and their families as his parting wisdom, how important it is to live life using both hands. We can be a more gentle people, take more care and cherish moments gently. I will always remember the stillness in Duke's beautiful chapel that day as everyone in attendance drank in his words.

I have worked in the medical profession for over forty years and in just everyday communication with patients, I notice their hands. Whether I am exchanging paperwork, shaking a hand or holding one, it says I understand and care about them. I have often thought of, especially in our more elderly patients how many tears were dried, how many babies were bathed, how many meals were prepared, how many foreheads were soothed when illness fell, and how many hands were held in prayer through times of trial and sadness. Our hands are the tools to teach and express love, charity, compassion and joy. May the years place their mark in magnificent ways upon yours.

CHAPTER TWENTY

Going The Distance ... And Then Some

Most of us live very full and busy lives that encompass many different aspects to which we are drawn and involved. Some of those elements are marriage, dating relationships, raising children, careers, friendships, caring for aging parents, service to others, our faith affiliations, listening to and not judging someone you love, loving and caring for a family member or friend who is faced with a terminal illness, forgiveness, never forgetting to smile and lend a listening ear to someone that just needs a friend. These are just some of areas that have come to my mind. Every aspect of our lives, when you think about it, requires going the distance if you are seeking to make an impact for the best possible good. Sometimes, when you feel like you have nothing else to give, just remember the person or the purpose and it will be easy to "go the distance... and then some." Often it is just one more mile, a hand to hold, a warm hug, an extra dose of compassion, understanding and loving unconditionally that will make all the difference.

CHAPTER TWENTY ONE ♡ *Just Where You Are*

Have you ever felt as though you seem to be standing still while the rest of the world is moving all around you? Each one of us has a unique set of circumstances that are a real part of who we are, and they can contribute to how timely things may happen for us. While some may seem to be reaching their goals sooner, others may be on a slower path for any number of reasons, and theirs will be realized at a later time. Most importantly, you are moving at a pace that is unique to YOU. Your hopes, dreams, and goals are all within reach. Maintaining a positive attitude and continuing steadily down your own path, you will arrive where you are meant to be.

CHAPTER TWENTY TWO ♥ *Grace*

If we were able to meet together and share our philosophies of life, most likely they would all be somewhat different. I wonder… how do we accept defeat, how do we win the race with humility, will we always be glad to share what we have with others, will we see the magic and the miracles in every day, or will we have patience and dignity to wait for the answers we hope will come? These, and so many other circumstances have the ability to define us.

Life for many of us is one big test, followed by even greater lessons learned. I believe it all comes down to *grace* and how we accept each lesson and apply it in our daily lives. I personally know this to be true from the deepest part of my heart. The tender gift of grace is given to each one of us as a result of the defining moments in our lives, and often when we are in the middle of the most difficult and trying times.

I would like to share a story with you of the ultimate gift of God's grace I received in my life, in 1983.

In the chilly month of February, 1983, my youngest daughter was born, beautiful, healthy and on time, and we named her Chelsea. Three weeks after her birth our lives were about to change drastically. It was bedtime in our home, and my three week old baby girl would not have any part of going to sleep, so I picked her up from her cradle and cuddled her late into the evening. I watched her as she peacefully slept in my arms and all of a sudden, her tiny arms flailed in the air and she stopped breathing. Our instinct was to gently shake her to alert her to breathe, and thankfully she did.

Following this frightening episode she was admitted to Children's Hospital, Los Angeles where she spent a week having tests. At the end of the week, it was a unanimous diagnosis by all of the doctors involved in Chelsea's case, that she had experienced Near-Miss Sudden Infant Death Syndrome. We were numb and frightened, but so very grateful we still had our precious baby girl. Home from the hospital with our one-month-old, we felt we were ready for monitors and alarms that would sound all throughout the day and night to alert us if she would stop breathing. It was a time of high anxiety mixed with fear that it might happen again, and would we be so fortunate the next time. We had wonderful pediatricians and counselors that helped us through this time, and I will be forever grateful to each of them.

Three weeks after we were home we had settled back into the process of living, with our three older children needing a normal family life again. It was early evening and dinner was cooking on the stove. Chelsea was in her infant swing near me and as I glanced at her, I noticed she was turning a light blue. Fear I had never felt before swept through my body. Oh no… it was happening again and she was not breathing at all. We worked on her tiny body until there was a shallow breathing sound, and I called the paramedics. It seemed like an eternity until I heard the sound of their siren coming up the winding hills of La Crescenta to our home.

I remember holding her in my arms looking up at the stars in the sky and pleading to God not to let her die. Once in our driveway, the paramedics assessed her and we were rushed to Children's Hospital again. I remember the kindness, warmth and compassion from the paramedic I was sitting next to on the ride to the hospital. I felt in my heart that night that Chelsea would live. And, she did.

After another week in the hospital and more tests, the diagnosis remained the same. We were discharged to go home and continue living and to do just as we had done before, always exercising every caution with this syndrome. Through prayers and blessings from our church, there was never another episode in Chelsea's little life. She remained on the monitor for a little over one year.

It took me many seasons to get over this traumatic time in our family, but eventually I did, with many helpings of God's grace.

CHAPTER TWENTY THREE ♡ *A Welcoming Light*

Up a meandering road in Glendale, California, lined in giant oak trees, was my childhood home. In the evening our porch light was always on, especially if someone in our family was expected. In my teenage years this light took on a special meaning to me and has remained a beautiful part of my memories. That soft, shining light was a welcoming beacon, and spoke volumes to me that my family loved me and was waiting for my safe return. In sweet comparison, I think of our Heavenly Father, whose light always shines for us on every step we take. He will continually make sure our lamps are full of oil as we seek His love and ask Him for guidance on this, our earthly journey. I know with a deep surety that we will never be lost if we follow Him.

CHAPTER TWENTY FOUR ♡ *A Time To Trust*

Trust is a word that emulates a golden bond... its vow and value is immeasurable. Whether this bond exists between two people, within a family or between countries, it is a most prized pact. When this bond becomes tarnished, it is very difficult to bring back its shine and worth. Unfortunately, sometimes it may take years or perhaps, never. Over time, it may become a healing process and one that requires soul searching, faith and the ability to forgive and ultimately, trust again. We can become vulnerable when we need to trust someone. However, if we do not exercise the value of trust we will never find the true meaning of joy and love. To find the secure and warm feeling of both and peace within, it may be time to trust again.

CHAPTER TWENTY FIVE ♡ *The Sweetest Treasures*

Over a year ago, I was in the process of an exciting move back to our beloved Balboa Island. Eighteen years before it became necessary for my children and I to leave our precious cottage (one of the originals on the Island), as situations in our lives had drastically changed. With a sense of tender adventure and hope that sometime in the future we might return to this charming place called home, we began anew. We learned that *home* was wherever we were together. As anyone knows who has ever moved, it seems to be a constant state of "going through things" and "weeding out." Each time we moved, more and more was given away. I give great credit to my children in that they held close to their hearts what meant the most and made sure everything else found a good home. Now that my children are all raised and have lives of their own, it was my turn to part with the "things" that were treasures of my own heart. The cottage to which I was moving was precious in its cozy smallness, but did not offer room for many of the tangible treasures that meant so much to me. Finding "new homes" through friends, and at other times just a heartfelt goodbye to these treasures, was the best I could do. What I have learned through many years of moving is this... what we love most and must bid farewell to, will live on in our hearts forever. These *sweetest treasures* will remain in my heart always.

CHAPTER 26 ♥ *She Adjusted Her Sails*

"She stood in the storm and when the wind did not blow her away, she adjusted her sails."
~ Anonymous.

This powerful quote was introduced to me during Breast Cancer Awareness month, 2015. It touched me deeply on many levels, because I know it is true. I watched my mother lose her battle to this disease, but in the process, *adjust her sails* to leave her family the gifts of love and courage.

I believe that as women, whatever trials we may have to endure, we are stronger than we think we are. As I am writing this book, I know that many of you are having to make changes in your own lives to lovingly accommodate others. And, it takes heaping amounts of courage, faith, and inner strength. We never know what we are going to be called upon to do in this life that will require more from us than we ever thought we had to give. You are most likely getting to know a little about me now as I have written of my own trials. A dear friend and our wonderful family therapist for many years, gave me the most sage advice when I was overwhelmed and felt I was sitting in my lowest trench. She told me to reach within myself for another helping of courage and it would see me through. I told her I was worried I may have used it all up, and she comforted me in saying, I had not. True to her advice it was never used up, even to this day.

Remember, we will continually arrange our beautiful sails for they will keep us on course for any storm we may need to face.

CHAPTER 27 ♥ *Be Still*

In this busy world we live in sometimes we just need to be still. It is only then that we can truly hear and witness the answers to our prayers, concerns and matters of the heart. In these quiet moments we are blessed with the assurance that God hears and answers our every prayer. And, in His perfect timing our answers will come in shining clarity. A beautiful Bible verse from Psalm 46:10, always brings a sweet peace to my prayers, knowing that God walks beside me and you… *"Be still and know that I am God."* In my own life, if I had not learned to be still and listen, many of the inspirations I have felt to write would have been lost.

CHAPTER 28 ♥ *Shining Through The Narrow Spots*

On my many walks around Balboa Island, I notice beautiful flowers in bloom. I am also aware how many plants and flowers grow through old wooden fences, as if determination to shine and bloom was their quest! Many years ago our family was moving from the beautiful, quaint town of La Canada, California. Before our move, I wanted to say my goodbyes to many friends and the shopkeepers I had grown to love as well. In a darling store I often found myself in, the owner told me through my tears, "Don't be sad, just bloom where you are planted." I have remembered her wise words of comfort for me from that day forward. Each one of us have the opportunity to choose our feelings, even if our circumstances are different than what we had hoped.

Sometimes in the smallest of gardens come the most beautiful flowers. May we choose to shine through life's narrow spots.

CHAPTER 29 ♡ *Newport Skin Cancer, 1100 Quail Street, Suite 102, Newport Beach, California*

This address happens to be where most of my hours are spent, Monday through Friday. This is where I work and where many patients have blessed my life through the eight years I have been fortunate enough to have this "calling." Even though I have many duties here that constitute a job, it is my interaction with the patients that walk through our doors who have touched my life. They have taught me compassion to its deepest degree. I will never doubt that God puts us where we are meant to be, and it is up to us to magnify that special place.

A wise patient one day leaned forward at my desk and whispered, "Always love what you do honey, and I can tell that you do!" Through the years I have said a tearful goodbye to many of these lovely patients. I am a better person today for knowing so many of them, many of whom have passed away. Their gifts of courage, grace, and love will live on in my heart always. May you love where you are, and magnify the gifts you have been given which truly make you unique, and able to leave your mark in the world.

CHAPTER 30 ♥ *Footprints*

Often times when I walk along the wet sand on the beach, I am in awe of the footprints I see. I wonder to myself... do they belong to a weary traveler, or to someone sorting out their life, a happy couple in love, or a lonely husband who has just lost his wife? I know this with a real surety, we are never alone. Our loving God walks beside us every day and He is aware when our footprints are lighter or heavier. For many years a single parent, it was my greatest comfort to take walks on the beach whenever I could, and talk to God. He listened to my fears about raising a family of five children, and praying I would get it right. I continually prayed for His grace, tender mercies and His guidance. And, somehow, after my walk had come to an end for that day, and the spray from the ocean had refreshed and recharged me, I knew God had heard my prayers and would bring me the answers I needed. Had I ever looked back on those walks when I was very depleted and reaching for God's hand, I don't imagine I would have seen my footprints, as I know He carried me.

CHAPTER 31 ♡ *Chasing Happiness*

As I look back on the years I have lived thus far, I realize that happiness came in many different phases. In my early years it was the small things that, if I could only have, would make me the happiest little girl on earth! As I grew up, bigger things!! As the years matured me, I have learned this and hold very dearly to these words... *It was the pursuit of the dreams, goals and the "finish line" that brought the greatest joy and happiness, and not "things" anymore.* All along, the journey was about learning the true meaning of happiness and living it every day.

CHAPTER 32 ♡ *When Only The Heart Speaks*

Each of us is going to encounter the loss of loved ones eventually in our lifetime, as it is a part of our mortal experience to have joy, pain, and sadness. The agony of loss is shuddering and the void is everlasting. However, the gift of time has its balm of healing which over an undetermined period for each one of us, can replace the great sting of death with our everlasting memories.

Many years ago both of my parents were diagnosed with cancer. Immediately, my mind was swirling with so many questions, mainly... how long will we have them... would we see another Christmas together? After all the questions, I somehow just went numb. It was an overwhelming time to wrap my head and my heart around. In what seemed like the blink of an eye, we lost them both. My last minutes with them filled my heart with the most precious and everlasting memories I could have ever hoped for. Many of our moments were in silence, when our unspoken words filled the room with so much love, and a sweet and peaceful feeling of what would await them in Heaven. I learned a most precious life lesson in those fragile last days. *The times when only your heart speaks, the soul of your loved one is listening.*

CHAPTER 33 ♡ *"It Won't Always Be This Way..."*

From the time I was a little girl, I remember these comforting words from my angel mother... "It won't always be this way." Her words never failed to calm me and always made any situation better. Now, so many years later, I use these same words to comfort my own family and dear friends. Whatever we may be healing from, hoping for, in the midst of, feeling worried or sad about, making decisions regarding, or any other feelings that may be stirring within us, time has a way of improving. What we feel at the time may never look any brighter, somehow will. It is a blessing that time, a good helping of patience, faith, and remembering these wise words will help see us through most anything. I personally know this to be true. Remembering some very trying years in my own life, I can now see the truth and the wisdom in my mother's words. Sometimes you have to pass through the storm, no matter how long it lasts, in order to feel the sun on your face and feel whole again. You will, I promise.

CHAPTER 34 ♥ *The Mighty Oaks*

Growing up I was fortunate to live in a neighborhood that was laden with beautiful oak trees. Their ever present energy and strength were a constant presence as I remember those years in my life. When the heavy winds came they were resilient, and because of their deep, widespread roots they were anchored in place. Year after year they never changed, even though so many things did around them. Many years have passed since I left that wonderful childhood neighborhood. Through the years, whenever I am surrounded by the greatness and beauty of these majestic trees, it gives me peaceful time to reflect about the unwavering strength it takes to get through life. Just as the roots grow deep within the oak tree, so must the values, love, and courage run deep within us. And, their branches ever reaching for the sun they need to sustain life, reminds us that we may reach to the Heavens in gratitude for God's abiding love each and every day.

CHAPTER 35 ♡ *Motherhood*

She was the fabric of our home. She set the tone for the rest of my life. She was my best friend. She was my mom. The most influential part of my life's story was the love I received in my home growing up. It became the cornerstone to what I strived for as I was raising my own family many years later. This story is not unique, but the sweetest blessing from God to women who are raising their families, a true calling... *motherhood*. It is not always easy, but the rewards far outweigh the sleepless nights. A mother holds within her the many gifts she will need to help her children on their life's course. One of my greatest gifts was the gentle "nudge" I always felt when I needed to inspire, intervene or just listen to one of my children when they needed me, or sometimes, when they thought they didn't! This "nudge" has never failed me to this day.

God Bless our mothers and the many who are not mothers, but have made an inspiring difference for good in the lives of others.

CHAPTER 36 ♥ *Your True North*

In the shelter of hushed and magnificent moments, we may feel answers resonate within regarding thoughts or questions we are contemplating. In the noise and commitments of everyday living it is often next to impossible to find clarity when we are seeking it. Personally, my greatest resource of direction is prayer. It is my *true north* that leads, guides, and comforts me every day of my life. Whatever quiet moments you may seek are yours alone. Eventually the heart, mind, and might will come together and bring the answers you are longing for.

CHAPTER 37 ♡ *Bailey! Bailey! Bailey!*

How do I begin to write about my furry, best friend? Her name is Bailey. If any of you have seen the movie, *A Dog's Purpose*, she shares this sweet name throughout the movie. At the time of writing this book she is nearing fourteen years of age, and has the energy of a puppy most of the time. She is my darling little companion! There are no words to express how she has touched my heart ever since she came into my life. She was a true gift to me just a few weeks after she was born, and she has remained so every day thereafter. She has watched the sweet furry companions in our family cross over the Rainbow Bridge and now, she lovingly has taken on the lead. I work long hours in a doctor's office, but her love and excitement never changes as we meet at the end of the day at the front door of our little cottage. Our walks are a gift to each one of us as she prances, nose up in the air, smelling all the fragrances the ocean brings. She snuggles next to me as I write, sits by me when I say my prayers (head bent down) and waits for me all day long until I return so we can do this all over again.

What do we learn from these little angels? We learn unconditional love wrapped in a wagging tail and wet kisses every single day. We learn to be happy with the small things and sometimes, just sitting and being still to cherish time with our little companions. We learn that rolling our windows down in the car does feel good, and turning up the music a little louder makes the ride even more fun, especially on a road trip. We learn that each day we have them is the gift they came here to give... their love, loyalty, and steadfast companionship. I have to believe that their unselfish example is for us to learn from and graciously give to others. *Oh! I love you Bailey girl!*

CHAPTER 38 ♡ *Friendships*

This is a golden word for many of us... if it resonates within you this way, you are very blessed. At an early age we learn the meaning of the word *friend*. As the years go by, these friends may come in or out of our lives for any number of reasons. Many of them will have left the most tender of footprints on our hearts, and they are prints that will never be erased. These are the friends that have taken our hand on the journey, when everything seemed impossible and their abiding love was the gentle light that helped us get home. I am grateful to say that I have been blessed with such beautiful and eternal friendships. I love you with all my heart.

CHAPTER 39 ♥ *One Kindness At A Time*

At this stage in my life I feel certain my "bucket" has reached overflowing many times, and the root is always the same—kindness. I am certain I share this beautiful and grateful feeling with many of you. And, I say this humbly as I recall the loving acts of service, words of encouragement, and prayers for me and my family over many years, just in living life itself. Our buckets become full not only when we receive, but when we give as well. When we reach out to others on a daily basis in small or grand ways, our own buckets fill one drop at a time. As we all have the innate desire to be loved, sometimes even a warm smile can make all the difference to someone else. It is my wish that we become aware of our sincere, small acts of kindness every day and remember that it is much greater to give than to receive.

CHAPTER 40 ♥ *Safe Harbors*

The word *harbor* can be defined as a place of security and freedom. I can't help but think of the people and places that have been a *safe harbor* in my own life. It is comforting to know that we not only have deep waters to drop anchor, but open arms that welcome us. At any given time, life can present us circumstances that can alter our destination. It is then we begin looking for the lights in the harbor and their welcoming love that will guide us to safety.

CHAPTER 41 ♥ *Wish Big!*

As I live my life each day, I have learned to have dreams and follow them and, always WISH BIG! I begin my day with the sincere intention of finding exceptional moments wherever I may be. Often, those moments are just what I was wishing for, and other times, not quite! But, nevertheless, I have learned that whatever answer comes, it was meant for me to follow. I know this—the most important lesson is to receive the answer in gratitude and in finding "new lenses" to see things differently. This lesson has brought me to many beautiful surprises that I would have never known to wish for. May you find your own remarkable discoveries in the midst of wishing big!

CHAPTER 42 ♥ *Be Brave Today*

We really never know the events within a day which call upon us to be brave. When will we need to draw from our own supply of inner strength and our personal reservoir of courage? From many years of digging deep from within that tremendous wellspring, I wondered if at any moment it might be empty. I know with every part of me, that God has already made his overflowing deposit of bravery within each one of us. And, on any ordinary day, we may be sharing right where we are, a big serving of that courage with another person in their own hour of need. By simply being there, we are an example of God's grace. These experiences don't live on a "bucket list," they just happen, and we become stronger from them.

CHAPTER 43 ♡ *Hope's Promise*

As you have turned to this chapter, I want you to know that nothing is impossible. With every challenge there is growth, with every prayer comes an eventual answer, with every step you are that much closer to your personal destination, and after the storm you will see the rainbow. And, finally with hope never ending, you will find peace. When we take the opportunity to help instill hope in someone else, it is as if a soft light was turned on at dusk. We have unknowingly bestowed the greatest and most lasting gift of love. As we strive to see the soft light of hope glisten in our own lives, we can become the beacon to others in their quest.

CHAPTER 44 ♡ *Our Fellow Travelers*

On this road of life we meet many people whose destinations are different from ours, but whose basic intentions and values we have in common. These are our fellow travelers. We can make a difference for good on this "road" by showing compassion, charity, selflessness, and reaching out and giving of ourselves. When we are humble it is natural to bestow these gifts of self on others, even if another is unable to bring anything in return. May the journeys we take be full of fellow travelers, and our memories of them, sweet and unforgettable.

CHAPTER 45 ♥ *God's Unfailing Love*

God's love speaks to us every day in different ways, in new places, and often through other people. We may encounter this love in the faces of our families and friends we love dearly, in the comfort that comes during trying times, from the inspiration and answered prayers we have waited for patiently, and within the tender eyes of strangers longing for a friend. Having been the grateful recipient of this love many times throughout my life, I believe we are here on an earthly errand to love one another because of God's unfailing love for each one of us. As we live in the light of His perfect love and share it with others, we will never be alone.

CHAPTER 46 ♡ *The Pink Sweater*

Into each of our lives, at different times, come moments we will never forget. Sometimes, they can be just as little as a few words spoken. As I have written intermittently throughout the years, I work in a very specialized doctor's office where various forms of skin cancer are the focus of our care. We are so blessed to know and treat wonderful patients. I have learned much from their wisdom and kindness over the years and many of them will forever stay in my heart. One day a few years ago, I was visiting with a fine gentleman who carries in his own heart a beautiful love for his late wife. He gently volunteered memories he missed most. "Whenever my wife and I went to a restaurant," he recalled, "I would always carry her pink sweater, just anticipating she might get cold." Tears filled his eyes, and mine as well, remembering those times. Selfless love. My dear friend, if you happen to be reading this chapter, you are my hero. May we all look for the *pink sweater* moments in our lives to embrace those we love, and to create a sweet remembrance that will help to keep us warm when they are no longer with us.

CHAPTER 47 ♡ *Smell The Roses Along The Way*

Many years ago, before my beloved mother was at her end stage of cancer, we took a little walk together on Balboa Island. Every garden was full of summer roses spilling over and through white picket fences. I remember as if it was yesterday, we stopped so that my mom could smell one very fragrant rose, in particular. She said so lovingly to me, "Don't forget to take time to smell the roses." I knew she was giving me a pearl of wisdom before she died. At that time I was so busy raising my family, I could not imagine having a spare moment to do that, even though it sounded blissful. Now, over twenty five years later, my children raised, I do have time and it is very precious to me, especially when I am holding the hand of one of my grandchildren. I believe that when we take the time to honor God and His beautiful creations, it is the sweet fragrance of gratitude we are giving back. Now, each time I smell one of these beautiful roses, I look up and say, "Thank you Mom!"

CHAPTER 48 ♡ *Goodbye Summer!*

We are going to miss your sun kissed months on the beach, longer days and warm evenings to play, more cherished family time, ice cream cones and barbecues, and the sweet aroma of your luscious bounties. Your visit comes to a close with just the faintest feeling of a cool breeze as you open the door for Fall. Of all the four seasons, Fall is my favorite! I love pumpkins at my door, apple picking with my family, cooler days and crisp nights, the vibrant sight of red and orange leaves, baking pies and wearing sweaters. Most of all, this cozy season prepares me for the gratitude I feel so abundantly in the months of November and December. I believe that our seasons were perfectly placed in a Divine order. Fall, its shorter evenings, makes us turn to hearth, home, and family at the end of each day. Winter has us looking Heavenward as we prepare to celebrate in the month of December the birth of God's beloved son, Jesus Christ, and the eternal goodness He brought to this earth for each one of us. Spring, with her exquisite new beginnings, brings us hope for good things ahead.

CHAPTER 49 ♡ *Love Whispers*

A whisper is the most delicate form of communication, not only between two people, but in nature as well. It can be the faintest sensation of wind on your face that whispers an answer to a prayer, a secret shared between two people in love, or the sweet, pure confidence of two adorable children. However it may embrace you, hold it dearly in your heart, as it was meant especially for you, at that moment in time.

CHAPTER 50 ♥ *The Best Is Yet To Come*

We have all heard these words, *the best is yet to come* at different periods throughout our lives. Sometimes, this heartfelt delivery comes at a time of struggle, stress, or sadness. At others, it is said more lightly as a new year begins, or in having hope for new things wished for. None of us really know what lies ahead, but what we do know is with every fresh new day comes renewed hope. We have the great potential within us to be our best selves and in doing this, we will reach higher, have more understanding, and learn more patience for those things yet to come.

CHAPTER 51 ♥ *Look At The Hill, Not The Mountain*

I have found, it is the succession of *hills* we climb that prepares us for the *mountains* in life. The hills and valleys are the ups and downs in our lives, and are the teachers of inner strength and courage. Over twenty-five years ago, I learned firsthand of these, and I am continuing to be taught today. I learned that no matter what I had to face, there was always another helping of strength for me to draw upon. I continued to learn to look at what was immediately in front of me, and not too far down the road. By doing this, the trials and challenges that seemed to keep coming were less daunting, and before I knew it, I had climbed another hill. Today, I am grateful for that journey so many years ago, and for the loving hand of my Heavenly Father that held mine, every step of the way.

CHAPTER 52 ♡ *The Wedding*

When I began writing this book, I always wondered when I would know what the ending should be! After all these months, it became very clear to me. We can't plan the chapters in our lives, we can only learn from the life experiences within them. Hope being, to bring them alive for others so they can learn and grow to their deepest potential. On May 26, 2017 my youngest son Casey was married to his beautiful soulmate, Gabriella. There is a place in my heart that will always replay this very special day. Both Casey and Gabriella asked me to officiate their wedding a few months prior to their ceremony. The honor they bestowed upon me was magnificent. The ceremony I was left to write, gentle words of advice that would be in their forever, the tenderness and humor in marriage, all weighed heavily in my prayers every day for Heavenly Father's guidance. Once I invited God to take the lead, it all came into place. As their beautiful wedding day arrived, a day that was predicted to have rain, we welcomed a glorious sunny day! I will never forget the warm feeling course through me as the tender words God inspired me to write flowed from my lips and into their hearts.

As you have read through the pages I have written, we don't plan life, it happens to us. It is up to each one of us to learn from the lesson taught by the experience, whether happy or heartbreaking. As you reflect on the stories and the thoughts I have shared, I hope you take away that given any circumstance in life, you will eventually find peace and hope. It may take time, and a lot of patience, but it will come. And in the meantime, the person you are becoming will be unforgettable because of the grace you have exhibited.

Postscript

At the end of this book it seems only fitting that good news be shared. In Chapter Eleven I have written of Trials.

I wrote of the trial we faced with my oldest daughter, with the diagnosis of an inoperable brain aneurysm, on Easter Sunday, 2015. One and a half years wondering what each day would bring, but having faith to know somehow it would all be okay. And, daily prayers that she would live and continue raising her four beautiful children. We had our miracle on August 28, 2017. She had a successful surgery to contain the aneurysm by a renowned neurosurgeon at UC San Diego. Through a dear friend, Holly was introduced to him and the rest unfolded into a very successful surgery. We will always be grateful for this gifted surgeon and for all of the many prayers on Holly's behalf. God's overwhelming grace gave my daughter her life back. There are not adequate words to express my love, joy, and gratitude as her mother, I only know there were angels in our midst.

Gratitude

This is perhaps the most important page of my book. It is here I want to express my heartfelt appreciation and gratitude to those who have helped me in countless ways, in achieving this dream come true in the writing of *Monday Moments*.

My Heavenly Father, for His gentle loving guidance in my life and for listening to and answering my prayers for continual inspiration.

My Parents, who raised me in a golden childhood era, where their love and my memories have shaped my values and character to this day.

My Brother, the gentle giant. His love and shining example are a constant in my life every day.

My Children, for their endless love, tremendous support and unwavering belief in me. I love you with all of my heart.

My Grandchildren, for their every hug, "I love you Mimi," and every smile that melts my heart.

My Friends, for just being the special people they are, and for walking beside me on this wonderful journey.

Teri Rider, my outstanding publisher and friend. I had hoped to meet someone just like her when it was time to publish my book, and gratefully I did. Her patience, wisdom, knowledge and kindness are a blessing to me.

Rachel Leigh Photography, photographer extraordinaire. Her soft palette was just what I wanted on the cover of my book. It beautifully sets the tone for what has been written.

Monday Moments Audience, I thank you for allowing me to come into your lives each Monday morning, and it will continue to be my joy.

Bailey, my sweet fourteen-year-old Cockapoo, who magically came into my life when my youngest child went off to college. She has been my faithful little pal ever since, and always cuddles next to me whenever I am writing. She is truly an angel with four paws.

The Ending

My reading audience, on Friday night, June 9, 2017, sitting by a warm fire with a cup of tea, and my four-legged angel cuddling next to me, I concluded my gift of love to you. Bailey will forever be my good luck charm, who entered my life in a cardboard box when she was six weeks old! It was love at first sight and she has been my sweetest companion ever since that memorable day. Tonight, the fire crackles inside a charming one bedroom cottage on Balboa Island where we live. For many years during some very difficult times, I kept a vision in my mind and in my heart that one day I would again return to live on this most endearing island, find a charming cottage, and there I would write a book. That vision became a reality in the Spring of 2016. Ever since then, I have been writing this book of inspiration in the inviting little cottage I could only dream about. **Monday Moments** tells my story around the events which shaped my life for good. It is my hope the pages I have written will heal your soul, increase your faith, renew your courage, give the word gratitude new meaning in your life, and patience will become a virtue as you wait for things hoped for.

I am deeply grateful for my five beautiful children whom I love with all my heart, two loving sons-in-law, a lovely new daughter-in-law, five adorable grandchildren and my wonderful brother whose love and gracious heart has been a shining example in our family. Each of my children, in their own very special way, have been and continue to be a sterling inspiration to me. My dear friends whose loyalty and love for more years than I can count, have been my cheerleaders, my examples, and the soft and comforting light on the sometimes difficult trails on the path of life. To all of you, I express a warm and heartfelt THANK YOU for believing in me as I have written this book. There is a little memory of each one of you within these pages. I thank God for hearing my prayers every morning and night, whether I was on the mountain peak or in the deepest valley, He was always there.

In closing this sweet little book, I would like to leave you with my heart gifts as you continue on your own unique journey. Embrace each new day and look for the magic in it. Be a blessing in someone's life. Make your life extraordinary even in the smallest way. Be grateful for everything, even your challenges, as often they are our greatest teachers. Lastly, I pray that when you are reading this book, I will truly speak to your heart through what I have lived and believe to be true. May they be the simple, but guiding truths that will comfort you in your life.

God bless you, always.

My love,

Ann

ABOUT *Our Mom*

As I was compiling all of the blog posts from my archives, I realized what important roles all of my children had played, not only in my life, but in the creation of this book. When I asked them to contribute, they all agreed. Here are the words I will forever cherish.

My mom is unique in so many wonderful ways. But I am always especially in awe of her kindness and selflessness. She has always been the type of person who would give the shirt off her back to help another human being. And, I remember the day she literally did just that. She gave the sweatshirt off her back to help keep a homeless person warm. The sweatshirt was red. Looking back now it was symbolic of my mom's big heart. I recall the way she saw the person cold and in need. And, how she didn't think for more than a second before she took it off and walked it over to this person she had never met. What was particularly special about this act of giving was how long her kindness continued to help that sweet soul. I will never forget driving down the street months later and I saw this same person, pushing a shopping cart with all her belongings wearing my mom's red sweatshirt.

Love,

Holly

My mom has been a sterling example of love, gratitude and strength throughout my life. She has taught me that gratitude and kindness are always in style, and that showing love and compassion can turn a simple moment into a lasting memory. Throughout my life, there have been countless times that friends and acquaintances have commented on how genuine, warm, caring, and thoughtful my mom is. Her ability to find the right words to comfort and encourage is a true gift, combined with her ability to give her whole heart and unconditional love into everything she does. Thank you, Mom for being a continuous inspiration and showing me what's possible by living a life of love, gratitude and strength.

Love,
Heather

My mom walks with elegance and poise always wearing a smile that lights up a room. I am complimented daily on what a wonderfully warm and inspiring person she is. My mom is commonly referred to as the nicest person anyone has ever met, which is true. My mom is an unassuming warrior who battled through overwhelming odds as a single mother to make sure that her children were given every opportunity for success, and most importantly, made sure every day every one of her children felt loved. My mom makes me feel lucky everyday I am her son. My mom is my hero.

Love,
Brett

Dear Mom,

Thank you for teaching me to smile in the face of hardship and to believe in myself no matter what anyone says. Thank you for always making me feel unconditionally loved and appreciated. Thank you for laughing and smiling with me through my stupid jokes, and for reminding me that the world isn't ending even when I think it is. Thank you for being my best friend, because you were the best friend I could have ever hoped for. But mostly, thank you for being the most wonderful mother imaginable, because I owe it all to you, thank you. Two words that mean so little when comparing them to every little thing it is that you do for me. Thank you for the countless hugs. Thank you for the laughter, the smiles, the lessons, and reminding me that I'll always have somebody who loves me for who I am, flaws and all. You have shown me that it is okay to make mistakes, it's okay to cry, and it's okay to be who I am.

I can only hope to one day become half the woman you are; resilient, beautiful, and intelligent. You are the kindest person I know, full of love and encouragement and I am incredibly blessed to have had the opportunity to have that all my life. So, Mom, I love you so much, to the ends of the Earth and until the day I'm no longer walking on it.

Love always,

Chelsea

Hi Mom,

Since that magical day on Balboa's Little Island I have watched you continue to share your gift of Monday Moments uplifting all your readers, family and friends along the way.

Your gift with words has always shined through, from your legendary hand written notes and cards to what Monday Moments is today. You taught us the value of putting our thoughts down on paper, mailing our thank you's and the art of having 40-50 extra stationary cards on hand just in case you needed to send a few dozen gracious gestures to your friends. You always have this encouraging, positive tone that makes for a heart warming read. So proud of you and grateful to call you my mom.

Love you,

Casey

ABOUT *Ann Hales*

Ann was born and raised in Glendale, California. The daughter of a wonderful family, and memories of a golden childhood era have shaped her character and values today. From her early years, Ann loved writing, whether it was letters from Girl Scout camp, keeping a diary or long letters to her grandparents who lived in Illinois, where she spent many summers. That passion stayed with her as she raised her own five children. A few of the ways she expressed her love through writing to her family were letters on birthdays, notes of love in their brown paper lunch sacks, words written of encouragement and inspiration to ease homesickness as they were away at college, and journal writing. For many years a single parent, Ann has drawn from her own inner strength, and life's experiences to reach out to others and bring them insight, comfort and a positive attitude through her words. Often, she had to "dig deeper" for another helping of courage during some difficult years, and those times brought her the gift of great inspiration as she writes today.

Ann is very grateful for her strong faith in God and coming through challenging times with grace. She says what she knows to be true is, "That which challenges us only makes us stronger to withstand the winds of life." She also acknowledges her faith as the cornerstone in the great blessing of raising her children. Being a parent, she feels, is the most important job one has, and you only have one chance to do it right! As her children were growing up she poured her love and belief into each one, that they could do anything they set out to do in life. And, she says, "I am a better person from what I have learned from them, and our closeness as a family is a gift to each one of us." Now that her beautiful family is raised, she finds this time of writing and reflection her passion.

Ann works full time for two renowned skin cancer (Mohs) surgeons in Newport Beach, California, and loves her occupation. There she is able to interact with patients and bring them comfort and knowledge of the surgery they will require, and she finds her days greatly fulfilling. On weekends she loves spending time with her family and her five darling grandchildren. She also enjoys cooking, entertaining, gardening, and lots of great walks around Balboa Island with her little dog, Bailey.

So, how did *Monday Moments* come to be? On a sunny summer day, June 7, 2009, Ann was relaxing and reading a book on Balboa's Little Island. Her youngest son came by to visit and during their conversation, his encouragement and enthusiasm for her to continue writing and inspire others sparked a real sincere interest in Ann. She always felt the experiences in her life thus far had not been by chance. The insight she had gained was a gift and the opportunity to write and share with others, a great blessing. Her thoughts turned to writing a weekly inspirational thought and quickly its name became very clear to her. From her beach chair that very day and with notebook and pen in hand, Ann's heart and mind became one and took flight on an inspirational journey. Along with this was uncompromising love, enthusiasm, and encouragement from her family, friends and soon her *Monday Moments* audience, for whom she is forever grateful. The many thoughts she has written and will continue to write, are written with much love, understanding, compassion, and tenderness to what she believes are thoughts that run as a common thread through all of us. Ann's inspirational website, **Monday Moments** was launched in July, 2010 and she has been writing diligently ever since. She knew that one day she wanted to write a book for the public. With heartfelt determination and knowing her life's experiences weren't all for naught, this book was written with love in a charming little cottage by the sea.

Dear Reader,

Thank you for reading my book, I truly hope you enjoyed it and will find a passage or two that warmed your heart. I love getting your letters so please email me at ann@ mondaymoments.com, and visit my website to subscribe to my Monday Moments Blog, where I post messages like these every single Monday. You are now part of my family and I hope you will visit often!

Ann

www.MondayMoments.com